Colors, Shapes & More

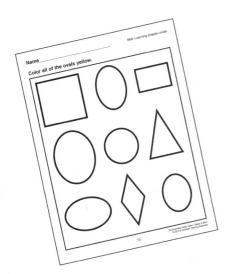

Written by: Aaron Levy & Kelley Wingate Levy

Illustrated by: Karen Sevaly

New York • Toronto • London • Auckland • Sydney
Mexico City • New Delhi • Hong Kong • Buenos Aires

Teaching *Resources*

■ SCHOLASTIC

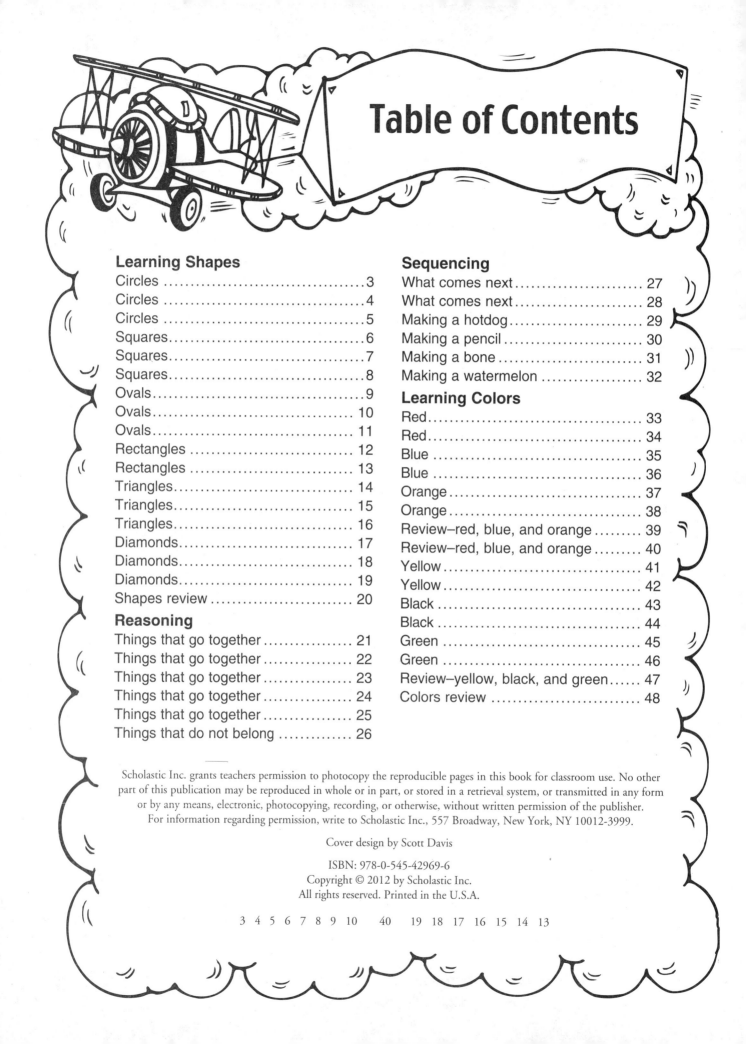

Table of Contents

Cover design by Scott Davis

ISBN: 978-0-545-42969-6
Copyright © 2012 by Scholastic Inc.
All rights reserved. Printed in the U.S.A.

3 4 5 6 7 8 9 10   40   19 18 17 16 15 14 13

Name_____

Trace and color the circles.

Preschool Basic Skills: Colors, Shapes & More
© 2012 by Scholastic Teaching Resources

Name_____

Color all of the circles red.

Preschool Basic Skills: Colors, Shapes & More
© 2012 by Scholastic Teaching Resources

Name_____

Trace the balls. Draw four more balls.

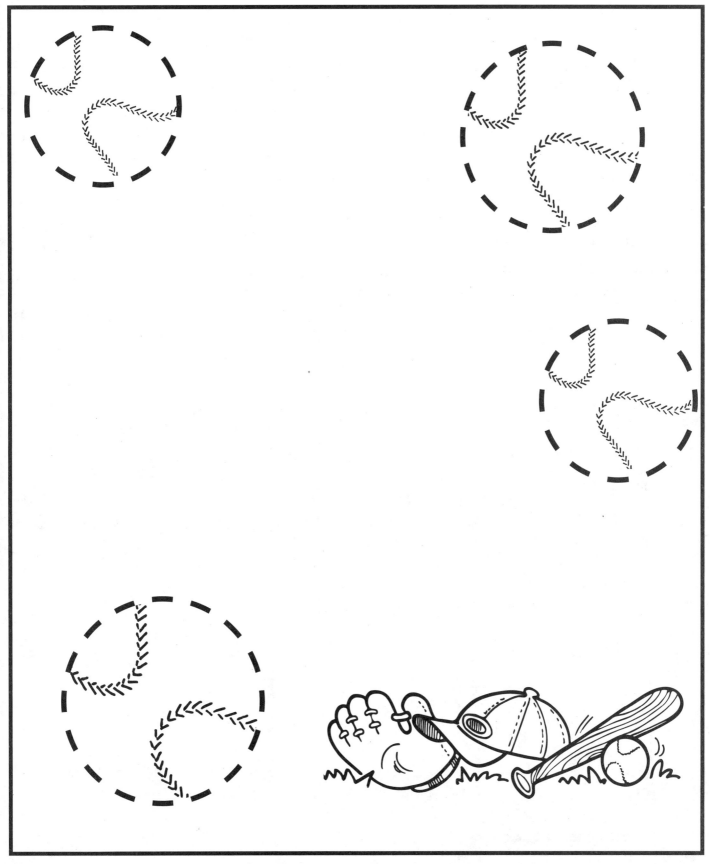

Name_____

Trace and color the squares.

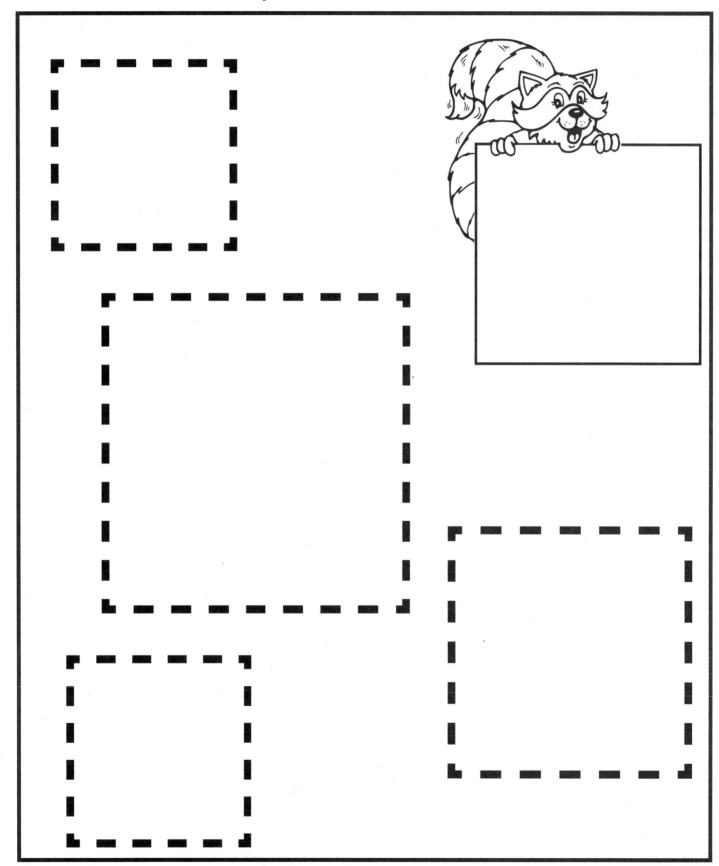

Preschool Basic Skills: Colors, Shapes & More
© 2012 by Scholastic Teaching Resources

Name_____

Color all of the squares blue.

Preschool Basic Skills: Colors, Shapes & More
© 2012 by Scholastic Teaching Resources

Draw four square gifts. Color each gift.

Preschool Basic Skills: Colors, Shapes & More
© 2012 by Scholastic Teaching Resources

Name_____

Trace and color the ovals.

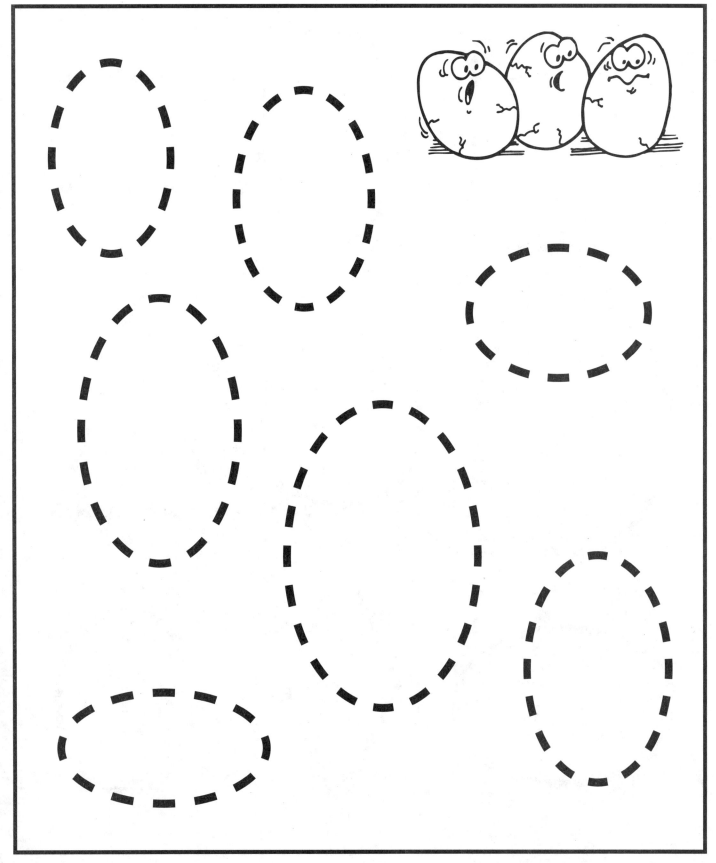

Preschool Basic Skills: Colors, Shapes & More
© 2012 by Scholastic Teaching Resources

Color all of the ovals yellow.

Preschool Basic Skills: Colors, Shapes & More
© 2012 by Scholastic Teaching Resources

Draw five oval eggs. Color each egg.

Preschool Basic Skills: Colors, Shapes & More
© 2012 by Scholastic Teaching Resources

Name_____

Trace and color the rectangles.

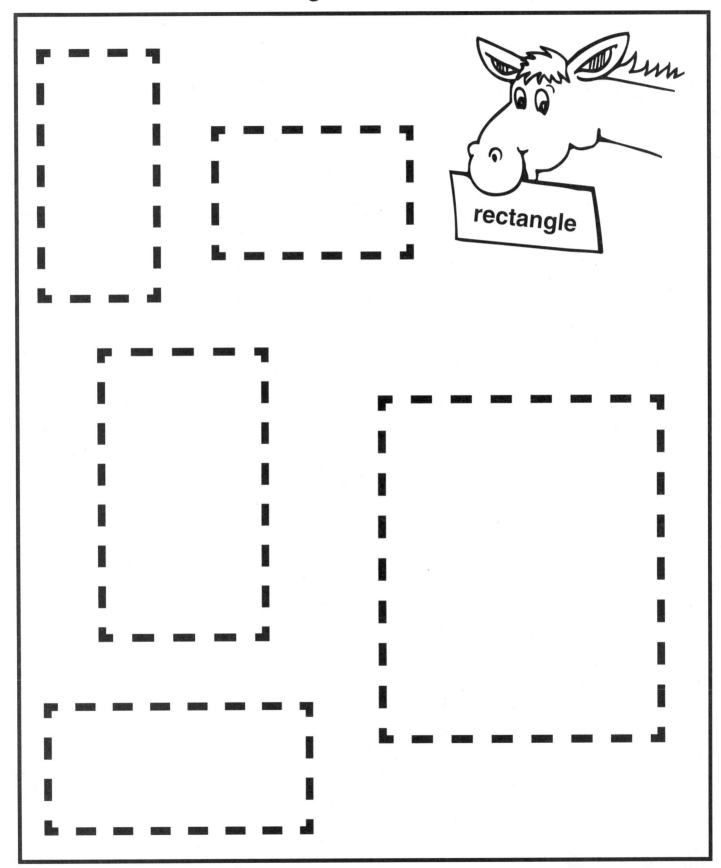

rectangle

Preschool Basic Skills: Colors, Shapes & More
© 2012 by Scholastic Teaching Resources

Trace each rectangle. Draw a rectangle in each box just like the first one.

Preschool Basic Skills: Colors, Shapes & More
© 2012 by Scholastic Teaching Resources

Name_____

Trace and color the triangles.

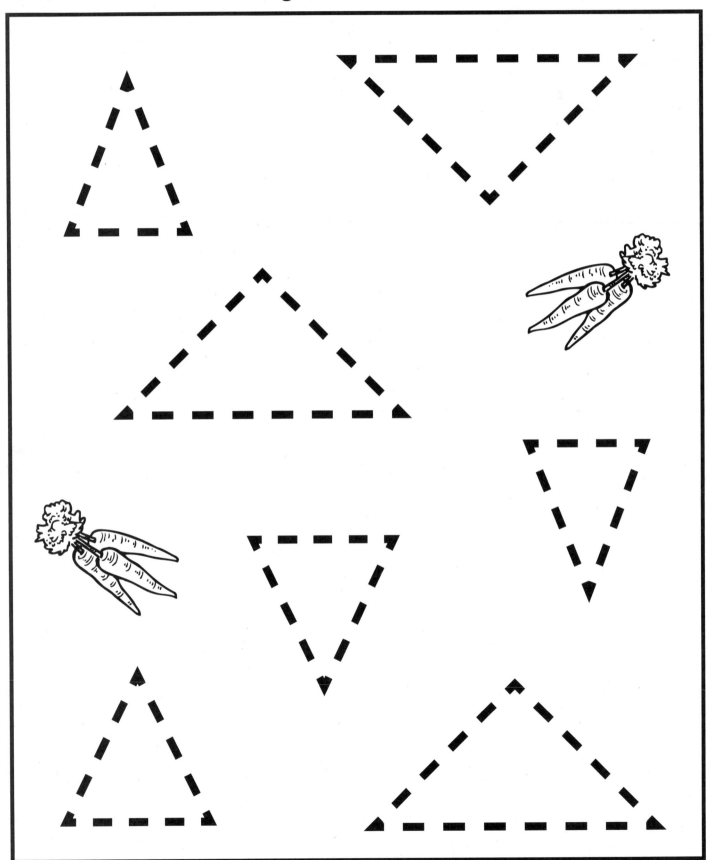

Trace the dotted lines to complete the triangle wings of each butterfly.

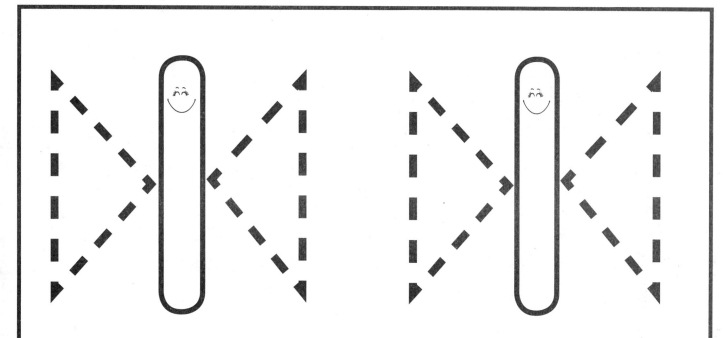

Draw butterfly wings for the butterflies below. Color the butterflies.

Name_____

Trace each triangle. Draw a triangle in each box just like the first one.

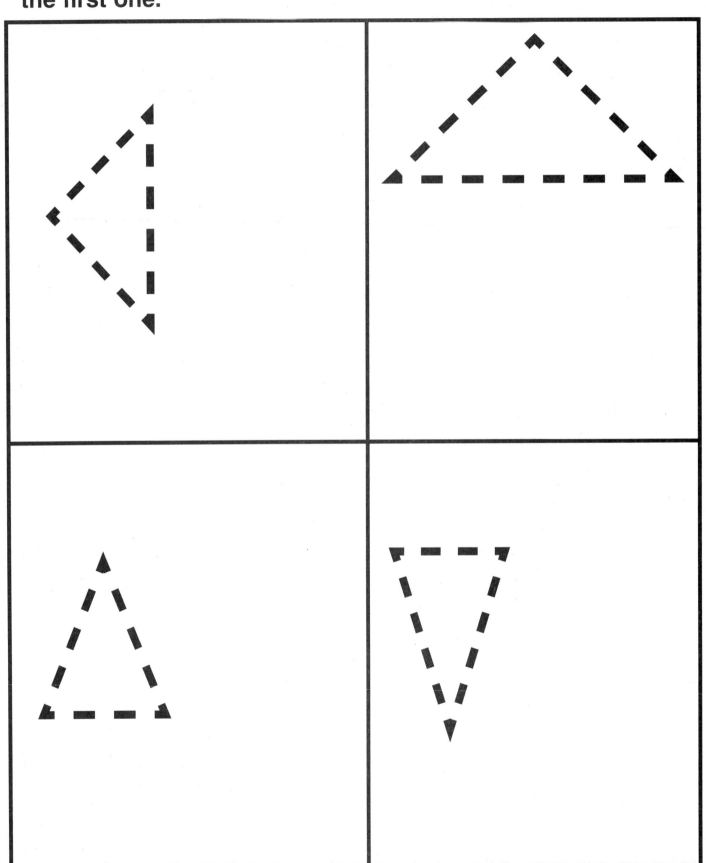

Name_____

Trace and color the diamonds.

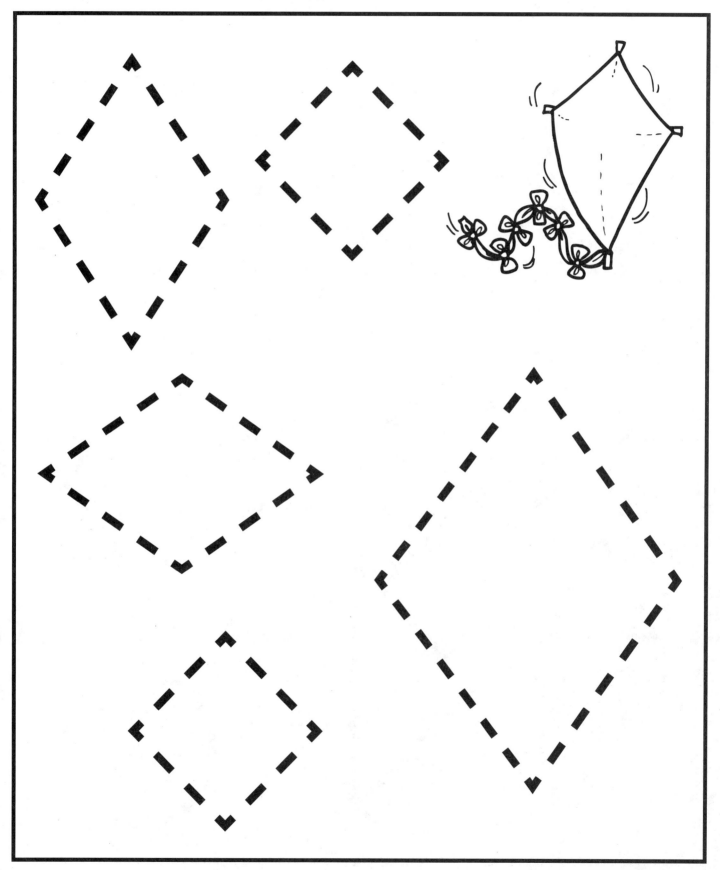

Preschool Basic Skills: Colors, Shapes & More
© 2012 by Scholastic Teaching Resources

Name_____

Color all of the diamonds green.

Name_____

Trace the dotted lines of each diamond to complete each kite. Color the kites.

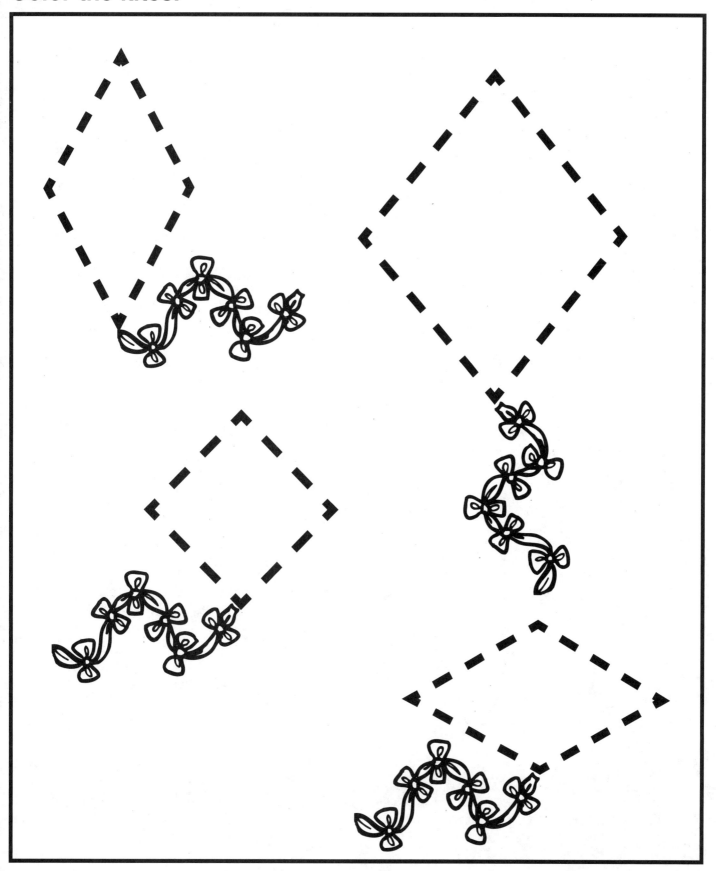

Preschool Basic Skills: Colors, Shapes & More
© 2012 by Scholastic Teaching Resources

Trace and color all of the shapes.

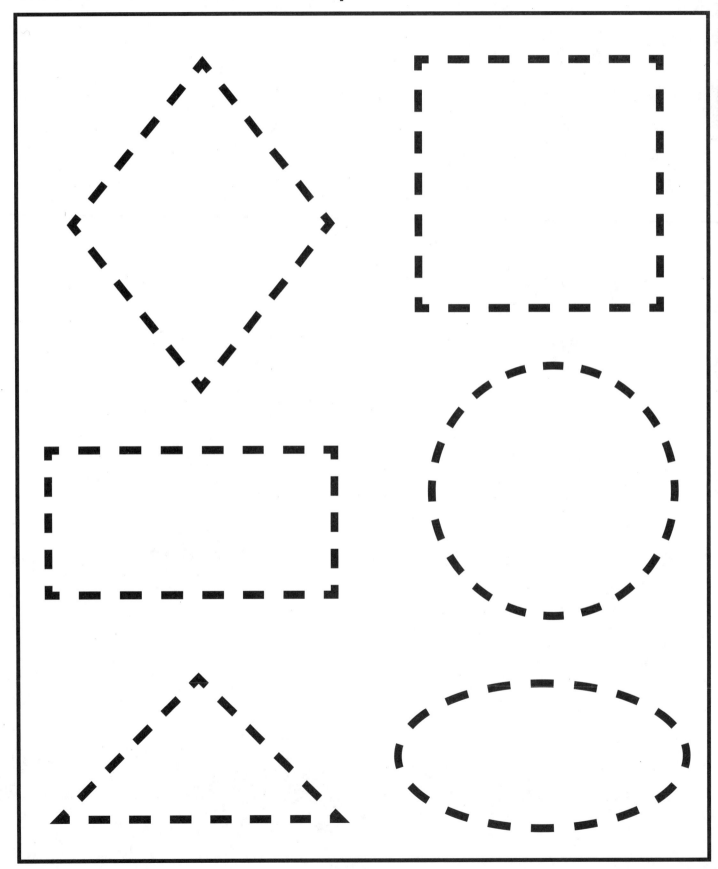

Name_____

Circle the three pictures that belong together in each row.

Preschool Basic Skills: Colors, Shapes & More
© 2012 by Scholastic Teaching Resources

Name_____

Circle the pictures that belong together in each box.

Name_____

Circle the pictures that belong together in each row.

   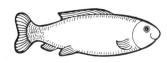

Name_____

Circle the pictures that belong together in each box.

Preschool Basic Skills: Colors, Shapes & More
© 2012 by Scholastic Teaching Resources

Name_____

Skill: Reasoning

Draw a line to match the pictures that go together.

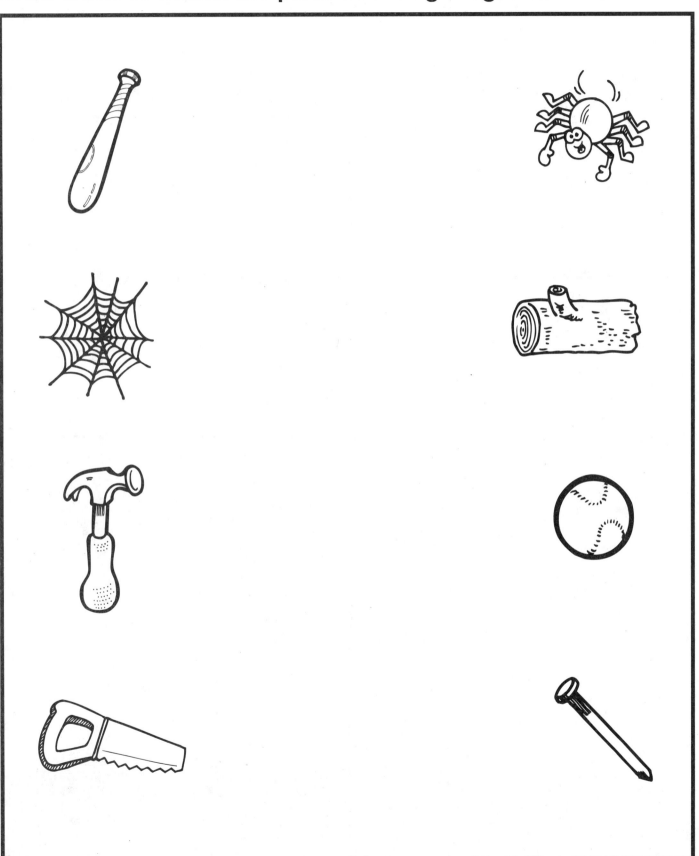

25

Preschool Basic Skills: Colors, Shapes & More
© 2012 by Scholastic Teaching Resources

Name_____

Put an X on the object that does not belong in each box.

Name_____

Draw what comes next in the box at the end of each row.

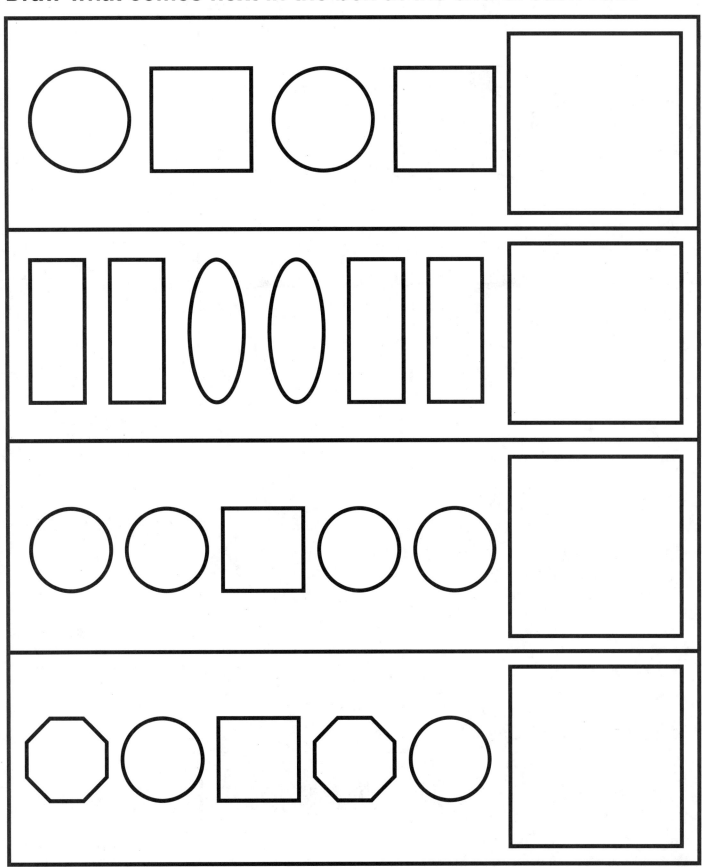

Name_____

Draw what comes next in the box at the end of each row.

Cut out the pieces of the hotdog. Paste them in the correct order to make a hotdog like the one pictured below.

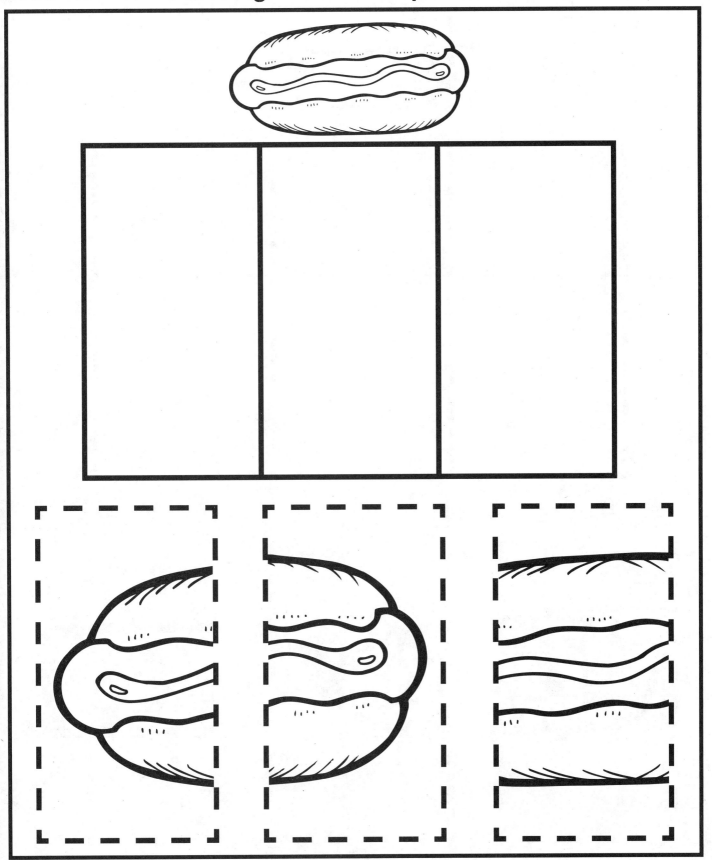

Name_____

Cut out the pieces of the pencil. Paste them in the correct order to make a pencil like the one pictured below.

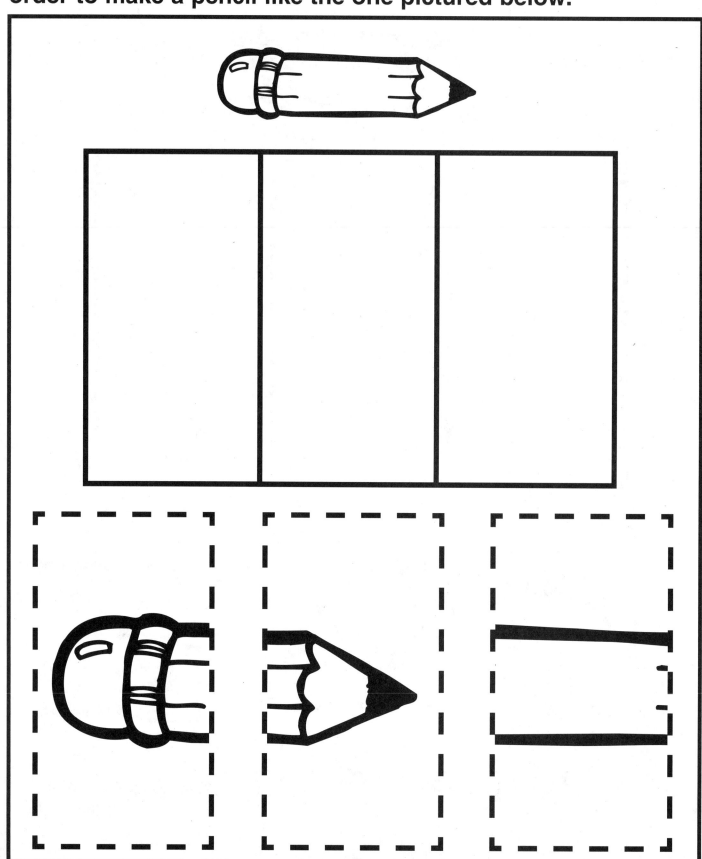

Name_____

Cut out the pieces of the bone. Paste them in the correct order to make a bone like the one pictured below.

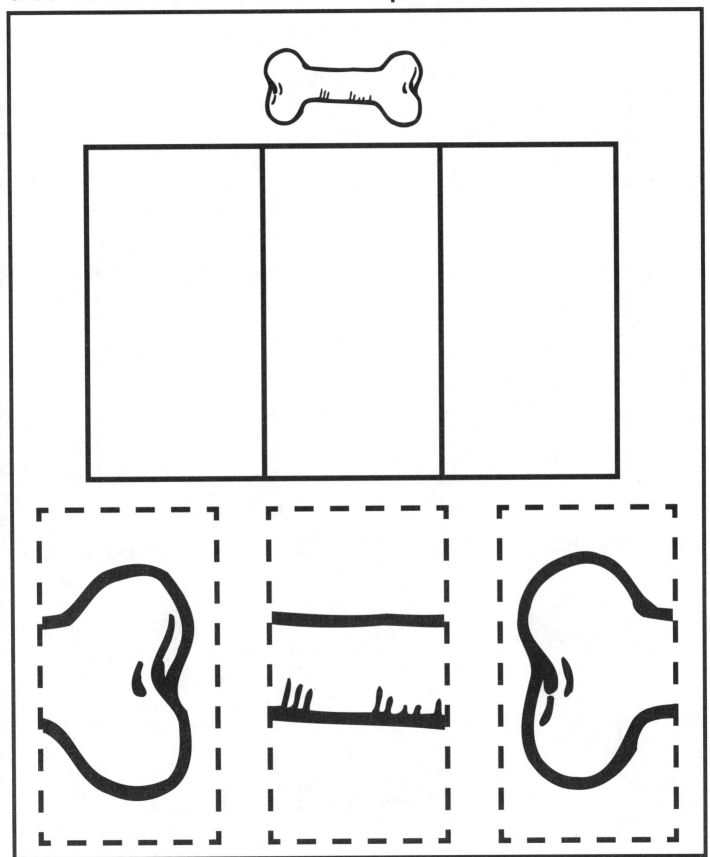

31

Name_____

Cut out the pieces of the watermelon. Paste them in the correct order to make a watermelon like the one pictured below.

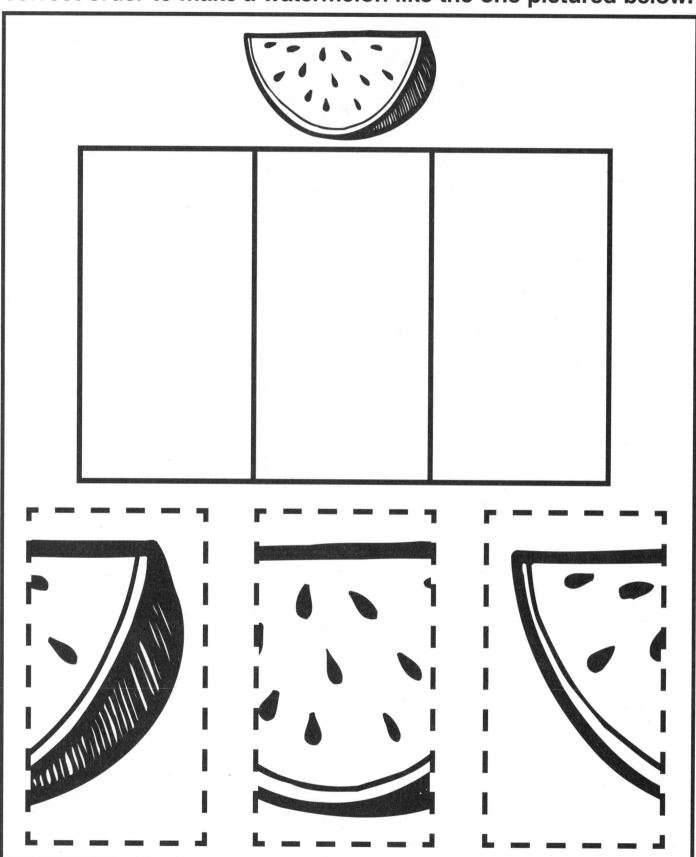

Preschool Basic Skills: Colors, Shapes & More
© 2012 by Scholastic Teaching Resources

Name_____

Trace the word *red.*

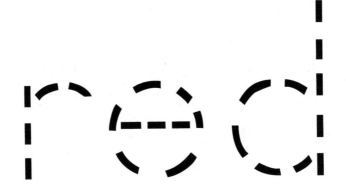

Color the pictures red.

Preschool Basic Skills: Colors, Shapes & More
© 2012 by Scholastic Teaching Resources

Trace and write the word *red*.

r e d

Draw and color a picture of something red.

Preschool Basic Skills: Colors, Shapes & More
© 2012 by Scholastic Teaching Resources

Name_____

Trace the word *blue*.

Color the pictures blue.

Name_____

Trace and write the word *blue*.

blue

Draw and color a picture of something blue.

Trace the word *orange*.

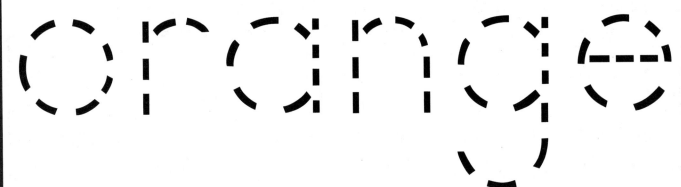

Color the pictures orange.

Trace and write the word *orange*.

orange

Draw and color a picture of something orange.

Preschool Basic Skills: Colors, Shapes & More
© 2012 by Scholastic Teaching Resources

Name_____

Color the pictures. Trace and write the color words.

Preschool Basic Skills: Colors, Shapes & More
© 2012 by Scholastic Teaching Resources

Color each picture the correct color.

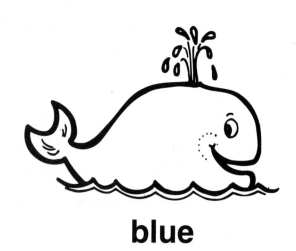

blue

blue

orange

orange

red

red

Name_____

Trace the word *yellow.*

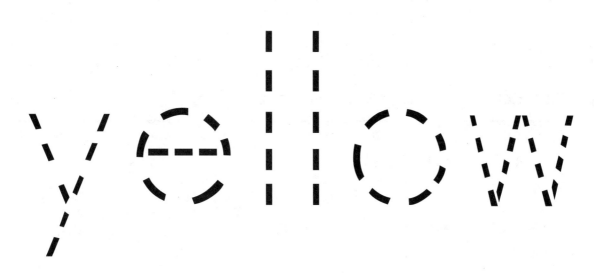

Color the pictures yellow.

41

Name_____

Trace and write the word *yellow*.

yellow

Draw and color a picture of something yellow.

Preschool Basic Skills: Colors, Shapes & More
© 2012 by Scholastic Teaching Resources

Trace the word *black*.

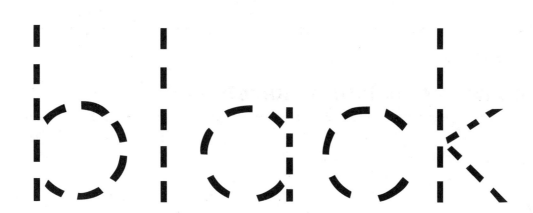

Color the pictures black.

Preschool Basic Skills: Colors, Shapes & More
© 2012 by Scholastic Teaching Resources

Trace and write the word *black*.

b l a c k

Draw and color a picture of something black.

Preschool Basic Skills: Colors, Shapes & More
© 2012 by Scholastic Teaching Resources

Name_____

Trace the word *green*.

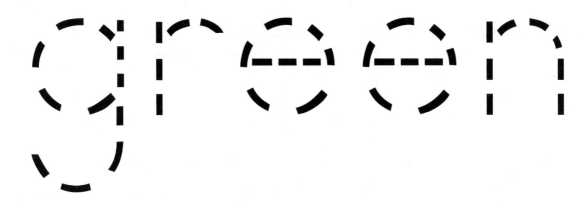

Color the pictures green.

Trace and write the word *green*.

green

Draw and color a picture of something green.

Preschool Basic Skills: Colors, Shapes & More
© 2012 by Scholastic Teaching Resources

Name_____

Color the pictures. Trace and write the color words.

yellow

green

black

Color each picture the correct color.

green

red

black

yellow

black

green

blue

orange

yellow

Preschool Basic Skills: Colors, Shapes & More
© 2012 by Scholastic Teaching Resources